D1544413

ECHINODERMS

by
Joanna Brundle

KidHaven PUBLISHING

Published in 2020 by KidHaven Publishing, an Imprint of Greenhaven Publishing, LLC
353 3rd Avenue, Suite 255, New York, NY 10010

© 2020 Booklife Publishing

This edition is published by arrangement with Booklife Publishing.

Written by: Joanna Brundle
Edited by: Holly Duhig
Designed by: Gareth Liddington

Names: Brundle, Joanna.
Title: Echinoderms / Joanna Brundle.
Description: New York : KidHaven Publishing, 2020. | Series: Animal classification | Includes glossary and index.
Identifiers: ISBN 9781534530577 (pbk.) | ISBN 9781534530300 (library bound) | ISBN 9781534531482 (6 pack)
| ISBN 9781534530515 (ebook)
Subjects: LCSH: Echinodermata--Juvenile literature.
Classification: LCC QL381.B78 2020 | DDC 593.9--dc23

PHOTO CREDITS

Front Cover – Jung Hsuan, franco firpo, 4 – aquapix, Tetyana Dotsenko, 5 – JGA, 6 – Maslov Dmitry, unterwegs, 7 – EpochCatcher,
NatureDiver, 8 – Jung Hsuan, NatureDiver, 9 – Dan Bagur, Rattiya Thongdumhyu, 10 – New Media and Films, Ponderful Pictures,
alexdrim, 11 – narupong sooknatee, 12 – DeeAnn Cranston, 13 – orlandin, Khoroshunova Olga, 14 – Ethan Daniels, 15 – Arto Hakola,
Cuson, 16 – Gloria Ann Roberson, 17 – elena moiseeva, Wet Lizard Photography, 18 – Randy Bjorklund, Dan Bagur, 19 – scubadesign,
Brandon B, 20 – Ethan Daniels, 21 – Gerald Robert Fischer, Rattiya Thongdunhyu, 22 – zaferkizilkaya, Ethan Daniels, 23 – Boris
Pamikov, Adel Newman, 24 – NatureDiver, 25 – Greg Amptman, 26 – zaferkizilkaya, dade72, 27 – OlgaLiss, e2dan, 28 – Milos
Stojanovic, 29 – Rich Carey, Scisetti Alfio.

Images are courtesy of Shutterstock.com, unless stated otherwise. With thanks to Getty Images, Thinkstock Photo and iStockphoto.

All facts, statistics, web addresses and URLs in this book were verified as valid and accurate at time of writing.
No responsibility for any changes to external websites or references can be accepted by either the author or publisher.

Printed in the United States of America

CPSIA compliance information: Batch #BS19KL: For further information contact Greenhaven Publishing LLC, New York, New York at
1-844-317-7404.

CONTENTS

Words that look like <u>this</u> are explained in the glossary on page 31.

THE ANIMAL KINGDOM

The animal kingdom is estimated to include over eight million known living <u>species</u>. They come in many different shapes and sizes, they each do weird and wonderful things, and they live in every corner of our planet. From the freezing waters of the Arctic to the hottest deserts in the world, animals have <u>adapted</u> to diverse and often extreme conditions on Earth.

Thousands of **new** animal species are discovered **every year.**

Although every species of animal is <u>unique</u>, they share certain characteristics with each other. These shared characteristics are used to classify – or group – animals. Animals are divided into vertebrates (animals that have a backbone) and invertebrates (animals that do not have a backbone).

Vertebrates include mammals, reptiles, amphibians, fish, and birds. Invertebrates can be divided into a <u>phylum</u> of animals called echinoderms. These include sea cucumbers, sea stars (also called starfish), sea urchins, sand dollars, basket and brittle stars, sea lilies, feather stars, and daisy stars.

ECHIN✪DERMS

WHAT IS AN ECHINODERM?

<u>Fossils</u> show that echinoderms have been around for a long time — over 500 million years. They were used by the Romans and ancient Greeks both in their medicines and as food.

There are around 7,000 species of echinoderms alive today, but there are also fossil records for around 13,000 species.

An echinoderm has an endoskeleton – this means its skeleton is inside its body. The endoskeleton consists of bony plates called ossicles, made of calcium carbonate – a lightweight, chalky substance. As an echinoderm grows, the plates of the endoskeleton expand to support and shape the body. Many echinoderms have spines that are also part of the endoskeleton and are covered by skin.

Echinoderms hatch from eggs that are either laid in water or carried on the female's body. Although most echinoderms are small – up to 4 inches (10 cm) in length or diameter – some grow very large. Sea cucumbers, for example, can grow to 6.5 feet (2 m) in length. The Midgardia Xandaros sea star is one of the largest species of sea star, with each arm measuring over 23.5 inches (60 cm). Many echinoderms, particularly sea stars and sea urchins, display beautiful, bright colors.

The sunflower star can weigh up to 11 pounds (5 kg).

ECHINODERM CHECKLIST

- 🐾 Invertebrate
- 🐾 Live only in saltwater habitats
- 🐾 Most lay eggs
- 🐾 Endoskeleton
- 🐾 Most have hard, spiny skin

BODY PARTS

Echinoderms display radial symmetry. This means that they can be divided equally around a central point (like a pizza cut into slices). Each is an equal, matching part. Feather stars and sea lilies have as many as 200 arms, which they use to trap food. Basket stars have arms that divide many times into a basket shape. The arms curl around food to direct it into the basket star's mouth.

Basket Star

Feather Star

Echinoderms have tube feet, which are tentacle-like structures, found on the arms of sea stars and on the undersides of sea urchins, sand dollars, and sea cucumbers. The tube feet poke through gaps in the endoskeleton and usually have suckers on the end. The suction allows the feet to be used for catching and holding prey and for gripping firmly to rocks or the ocean floor. Special tissue in the feet allows them to be extended or shortened, as required. Tube feet are also used for breathing.

The endoskeletons of sea urchins and sea stars often carry small, pincer-like structures called <u>pedicelleria</u>.

The tube feet of sea stars are arranged in grooves along the arms.

Sea Star Tube Feet

Echinoderms have a body cavity, called a coelom, which is filled with a watery liquid. Some of the major <u>organs</u>, including the digestive tube (gut), are found in the coelom. All echinoderms have a water vascular system. This is a system of water-filled tubes and storage chambers that fan out through the body and lead to the tube feet. Echinoderms use the water vascular system to move (see page 12), breathe, and transport food and waste around the body.

The mouth of the sea cucumber has feeding tentacles to help it gather food.

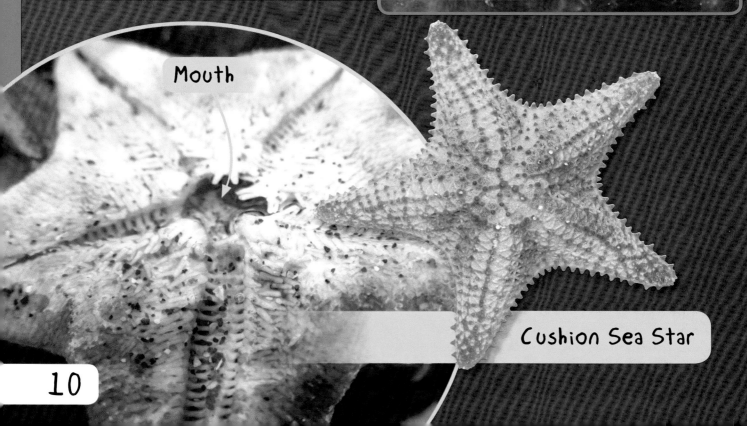

Mouth

Cushion Sea Star

Sea stars can push one of their two stomachs out of their mouths onto their prey. Digestive juices from the stomach then partly break down the food outside the body, before it is pulled back inside, where digestion is completed. Sea urchins feed using a system of muscles and plates, called Aristotle's lantern. The five teeth form a beak-like structure and are used for scraping <u>algae</u> from rocks.

Can you see the five teeth?

Many echinoderms, especially sea stars, brittle stars, and sea lilies, are able to regrow body parts, such as arms and spines, if they are lost to a predator.

This Nardoa sea star is regrowing an arm.

GETTING AROUND

Echinoderms move by pumping seawater through the water vascular system. This water is pumped into and out of the tube feet through an organ called the ampulla. This causes the feet to expand (get bigger) and contract (get smaller). It's similar to squeezing the air in a balloon from one part to another. Echinoderms move by expanding and contracting different groups of feet, so that as some stick on, others let go. The suction cups on the ends of the feet grip the seafloor, allowing the echinoderm to pull or push itself forward.

Spiny Brittle Star

Brittle stars are quick and agile, and move by wriggling their flexible arms in a rowing motion.

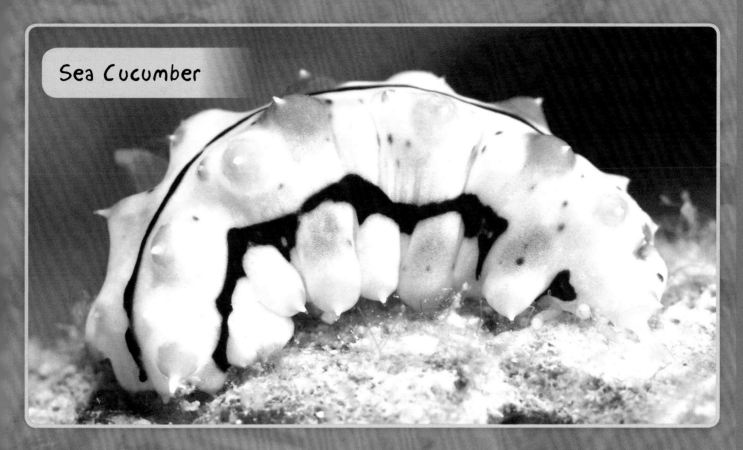

The ossicles in sea cucumbers are tiny and spread wide apart. This means that instead of having a rigid body, sea cucumbers are soft-bodied. This helps them to flex and wriggle, contracting and expanding their bodies so that they can move about and escape predators. They also have tube feet to pull themselves along, using their sticky tentacles as anchors. As well as using the tube feet on their arms to crawl, feather stars can also swim, using alternate up-and-down arm movements.

Most sea lilies don't move at all — they stand upright in the water on a stalk and waft their feathery tentacles to trap food.

13

PREDATORS AND ★ PREY

All animals can be sorted into groups depending on what they eat. The three groups are herbivores, carnivores, and omnivores.

Echinoderms can be herbivores, carnivores, or omnivores. Some, such as sea stars, brittle stars, and most sea cucumbers, are also classed as detritivores, feeding on dead plant and animal material.

Herbivores
Plant Eaters

Carnivores
Meat Eaters

Omnivores
Plant and Meat Eaters

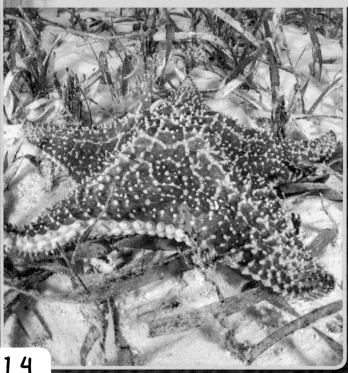

Omnivorous Oreaster Sea Star

Sand dollars and sea urchins feed mainly on algae. Sea stars are active predators, hunting mussels, clams, and oysters as well as crustaceans and smaller sea stars. Feather stars, sea lilies, and some sea cucumbers are suspension feeders, which means they catch food particles that float past.

14

Echinoderms have many predators, including crabs, fish, turtles, seabirds, octopuses, and sea otters. Seabirds, such as herring gulls, repeatedly drop sea urchins onto rocks until they break open. Some echinoderms are also <u>hosts</u> to <u>parasites</u>. The pearl fish lives inside the bodies of sea cucumbers, going in and out through the <u>anus</u> (bottom)!

Sea otters particularly enjoy sea urchins. They lay on their backs and smash the hard shells onto stones balanced on their tummies, eating the soft underside and carefully avoiding the sharp spines.

Humans are predators of echinoderms. Sea urchin eggs and sea cucumbers are commonly eaten in Asia. The fact that echinoderms are able to grow new body parts means that they are also useful to humans in medical <u>research</u>.

Dinner is served!

NATURAL HABITATS

Echinoderms only live in marine (ocean) habitats. They are never found in freshwater or terrestrial (land) habitats. They live in every ocean in the world. Although many species are only found in <u>temperate</u> oceans, some species are also found in the cold Arctic and Antarctic Oceans and in warm, tropical oceans, such as the Indian Ocean. Their habitats range from shallow waters at the tide line to the deepest oceans. Sea cucumbers have even been found at the bottom of the 6.8 (11 km)-mile-deep Mariana Trench in the Pacific Ocean, the deepest place on Earth.

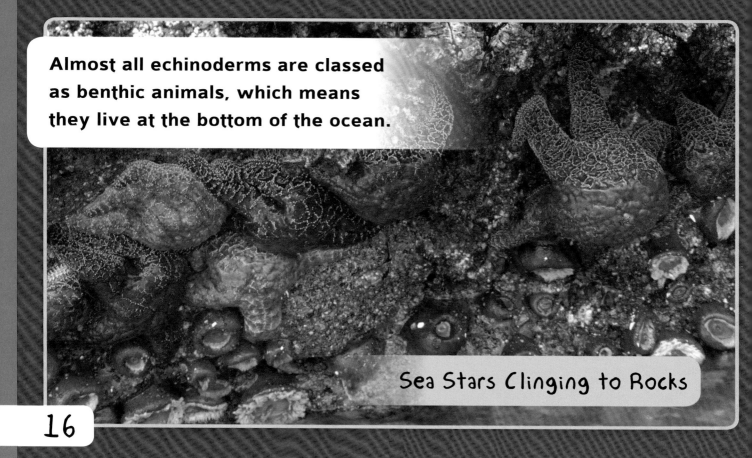

Almost all echinoderms are classed as benthic animals, which means they live at the bottom of the ocean.

Sea Stars Clinging to Rocks

Many species of echinoderm live on coral reefs, where sea urchins help to control the growth of seaweed, allowing the coral to flourish. On rocky shorelines, sea stars and urchins may cling to rocks. Some echinoderms use other animals as their home. Brittle stars, for example, sometimes live in large numbers in tropical sea sponges. Sea daisies live on pieces of waterlogged wood that have sunk to the ocean floor. Sand dollars live in sandy areas in shallow waters, burrowing their way into the sand to seek food and shelter.

Sand dollars have five sets of pores in a petal pattern that are used to move water into the water vascular system.

This brittle star is living in a vase sea sponge.

ADAPTATION

Adaptations are gradual changes in the body or behavior of an animal that help a species to survive in its habitat or to ward off predators. Some species of sea urchin, for example, have developed particularly strong endoskeletons and tube feet. These help them survive the pounding of waves onto rocky shorelines.

The purple sea urchin is commonly found on shorelines with strong waves.

Echinoderms are easily turned upside down but have developed a righting response: the ability to turn themselves the right way up again. Sand dollars burrow into the sand until they are standing upright on their rim, then allow themselves to fall over, the right way up.

Echinoderms have many adaptations that protect them. Some, such as sea stars, have substances called saponins in their body wall, which taste very unpleasant. Predators that take a bite get a nasty surprise! Sea cucumbers can protect themselves by shooting a mass of sticky tubes called cuvierian tubules outside the body to scare and tangle up predators. Sea urchins have strong muscles that move their sharp spines to protect against predators and to push themselves along.

Some echinoderms are <u>camouflaged</u> to blend into their surroundings while others display bright colors, probably to scare off or confuse predators.

This sea star is perfectly camouflaged against the sandy ocean floor.

LIFE CYCLES

The life cycle of an animal is the series of changes that it goes through from the start of its life to adulthood when it can reproduce.

Most species of echinoderm have separate male and female animals. The female releases millions of eggs into the water, where they are <u>fertilized</u> by the male. This process is called spawning. Most echinoderms spawn according to a yearly pattern, often in spring or summer.

Fromia Sea Star

Some sea stars lift the center of their bodies off the sea floor during spawning to prevent the eggs being trapped in <u>sediment</u>.

Fertilized eggs develop into larvae. The larvae feed either on yolk from the eggs or on tiny aquatic organisms. They gradually change, or metamorphose, over a period of a few days to several weeks into juvenile echinoderms. The water vascular system (see page 10) develops during metamorphosis. Sea cucumber, urchin, and brittle star larvae usually metamorphose as they swim and float along, before sinking and settling on the seafloor as juveniles. Sea star, feather star, and sea lily larvae attach themselves firmly to the seafloor before metamorphosis.

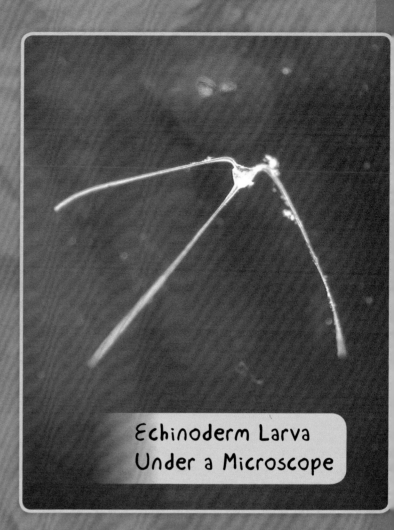

Echinoderm Larva Under a Microscope

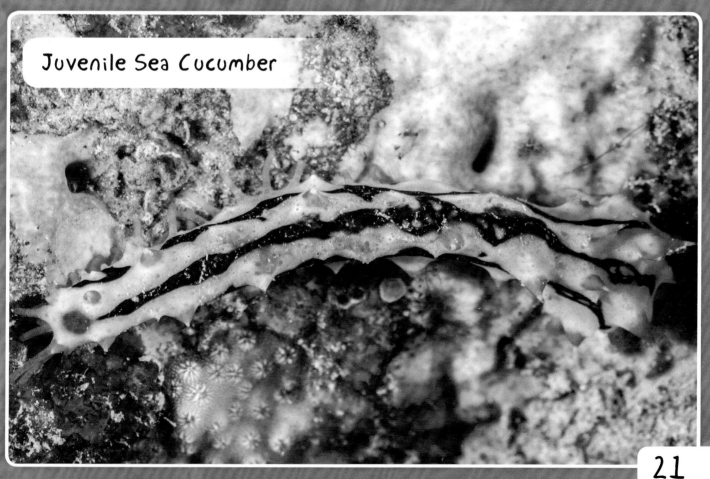

Juvenile Sea Cucumber

Some echinoderms can also reproduce by splitting the body into two or more parts (fragmentation) and then regrowing the missing body parts (regeneration). For this regrowing to be successful, certain body parts must be present in the lost pieces. Many sea stars and brittle stars can only regenerate if some part of the central disc, to which the arms are attached, is present. Sea cucumbers split down their entire length to eventually form two new animals.

Can you see where a new baby starfish is growing from the fragmented leg of an adult?

LIFE CYCLE OF A SEA STAR

REPRODUCTION

Female sea stars carry their eggs in pouches at the base of their arms. Millions of eggs are released during spawning. The eggs float until they are fertilized.

LARVAL STAGE

The tiny larvae are carried long distances by ocean currents. They feed on floating <u>plankton</u>. Many are eaten by whales and other predators.

ADULTHOOD

Sea stars reach adulthood and are ready to reproduce after two to five years, depending on their species. Their average life span in the wild is 35 years.

JUVENILE STAGE

The larvae gradually metamorphose into juveniles that look like mini adults. They hide under rocks until large enough to travel to find food.

EXTREME
ECHIN★DERMS

SUNFLOWER SEA STAR

Sunflower sea stars are one of largest and fastest species of sea star. They are often 24 inches (60 cm) across but can be as large as 3 feet (1 m). Sunflower sea stars can weigh up to 11 pounds (5 kg) and, thanks to their 15,000 tube feet, can travel at a speed of 3 feet (1 m) per minute – that's fast for an echinoderm. Like most sea stars, they begin life with five arms, but grow extra arms as they mature. Adults have between 15 and 24 arms, more than most other sea stars.

Sunflower Sea Star

The bones of our human skeleton are attached to one another. Together with our muscles, <u>tendons</u>, and <u>ligaments</u>, our skeleton keeps us upright and rigid. The endoskeleton of the sunflower sea star, however, has a few parts that are not attached to one another. This allows it to open its mouth very wide and also to expand its body, enabling it to devour large prey. It can, for example, swallow an entire sea urchin, its favorite food. It then passes the hard sea urchin shell, known as the test, out of its body.

Sunflower sea stars are found in a range of colors including purple, brown, orange, and yellow.

CROWN OF THORNS SEA STAR

The crown of thorns sea star is named for the thorny spines that cover the upper surface of its body. These spines are sharp enough to pierce the wetsuit of a diver and can cause severe pain and nausea in humans. The crown of thorns sea star feeds on fast-growing corals and can increase <u>biodiversity</u> by creating space for slow-growing corals. Population outbreaks, however, cause serious damage to tropical reefs such as the Great Barrier Reef. During spawning, between October and February, females can release 65 million eggs.

This crown of thorns sea star is eating mushroom corals.

The spines of the crown of thorns sea star can be 2 inches (5 cm) long.

SEA CUCUMBERS

Sea cucumbers are amazing! If attacked by a predator, some species can expel their internal organs, to startle and confuse the enemy. Within a few weeks, they are able to regrow a complete new set of organs. Their flexible bodies allow them to wriggle into thin, tight spaces to avoid predators. Sea cucumbers are able to change sex during their lifetime and breathe through their anus by drawing in oxygenated water. They are an extremely nutritious food, as they are low in fat and calories but high in protein.

Scientists have found that substances obtained from sea cucumbers may be useful in the treatment of human diseases such as <u>cancer</u>.

The colorful sea apple cucumber has a rounded body and a mass of feeding tentacles.

Sea cucumbers can grow much larger than the fruit after which they are named!

ECHINODERMS UNDER THREAT

Sea cucumbers provide a livelihood for fishermen and are an important <u>export</u> from many countries, especially to the US and China. Due to overfishing, numbers have dropped and over 370 species are now threatened. Of these, eight are classed as in danger of <u>extinction</u>. Some echinoderms are collected and sold live for use in aquariums. Endangered species reach high prices, and this encourages collection and smuggling. Sea urchins are collected by fishermen and divers for their eggs and their beautiful, colorful shells.

The removal of sea urchins by divers can harm coral reefs. Sea urchins eat algae and seaweed and stop them from growing out of control and destroying the coral.

Echinoderms are also threatened by damage to their habitats caused by human activities. Carbon dioxide is a gas that is released into the atmosphere when fossil fuels (coal, oil, and gas) are burned. Around half of the carbon dioxide produced dissolves into the oceans, making the water more acidic. Although some species are slowly adapting, this acidity makes it more difficult for echinoderms to produce their hard endoskeleton. Echinoderms are vital to the <u>food chain</u>, eating decaying matter on the seafloor and providing food as larvae, juveniles, and adults for larger aquatic animals.

Tiny plastic pieces can be swallowed by sea cucumbers and other echinoderms and could eventually find their way into human food.

Plastic <u>pollution</u> is found in all marine environments.

FIND OUT MORE

BOOKS

ANIMAL CLASSIFICATION

Discover and Learn by Steffi Cavell-Clarke

(Booklife 2017)

WEBSITES

BBC NATURE

www.bbc.co.uk/nature

Search under "echinoderms" for information, news, and videos.

MARINE EDUCATION SOCIETY
OF AUSTRALIA

www.mesa.edu.au

Search under "echinoderms" for information,
photographs, and fascinating videos.

NATIONAL GEOGRAPHIC

www.nationalgeographic.com

Search under "echinoderms" for videos, pictures, and articles.

MARINE CONSERVATION SOCIETY

www.mcsuk.org

Find out what is being done to protect our oceans
and how you can get involved.

GLOSSARY

adapted	changed over time to suit an environment
algae	simple plant-like living things that have no flowers, roots, stems, or leaves
anus	the opening at the end of the intestine through which solid waste leaves the body
aquatic	living or growing near or in water
biodiversity	the variety of living things in a particular habitat
camouflaged	disguised by traits that allow an animal to hide itself in its habitat by blending into its surroundings
cancer	a serious disease
export	something sent to another country in order to sell it
extinction	the process of being completely wiped out so that no living members of a species remain
fertilized	when reproductive cells are activated and develop into a new individual
food chain	a chain in which living things rely on the previous organism in the chain for food
fossils	the remains of prehistoric plants and animals that have been preserved in the form of stone, embedded or imprinted in rock
habitats	the natural environments in which plants or animals live
hosts	animals or plants in or on which a parasite lives
larvae	the young form of most invertebrates, amphibians, and fish that hatch from eggs but undergo many changes before looking like adults
ligaments	structures that join bone to other bone
organs	parts of an animal that have specific, important jobs
parasites	organisms that live in or on the bodies of other organisms and take their food from these other organisms
pedicelleria	pincer-like structures, used for defense and for removing unwanted particles from the body
phylum	a term used to group together living things that share the same characteristics
plankton	small and microscopic organisms that drift or float in the sea or in freshwater habitats
pollution	the act of introducing to the environment a substance that is harmful or poisonous
research	experiments and studies carried out to discover new facts and investigate new ideas
sediment	small pieces of a solid material, for example sand, that can form a layer of rock over time
species	a group of very similar animals that are capable of producing young
temperate	neither very hot nor very cold
tendons	structures that join muscle to bone
unique	unlike anything else

INDEX